OVERCOMING SELF-DESTRUCTION

This book tells about the Stop the Violence Movement—an unprecedented effort by young rap stars and music-industry colleagues to stop the violence at rap concerts and in their communities. The book contains lyrics, statements by the rappers, eye-opening statistics, letters from young people about their experiences of black-on-black crime, and the story of the Stop the Violence Movement itself.

STOP THE VIOLENCE

OVERCOMING SELF-DESTRUCTION

edited by

NELSON GEORGE

for the

NATIONAL URBAN LEAGUE

▲ ▼ ▲

PANTHEON BOOKS ▪ NEW YORK

Library of Congress Cataloging-in Publication Data

Stop the violence : overcoming self-destruction / edited by Nelson George for the National Urban League.

p.   cm.

ISBN 0-679-72782-5

1. Rapping (Music)—History and criticism.   2. Self-destruction.   3. Violence—United States.   4. Violence—United States—Prevention.   5. Inner cities—United States.   I. George, Nelson.   II. National Urban League.

ML3531.S76   1990   89-43235

303.6—dc20

Grateful acknowledgment is made to the *New York Times* for permission to reprint "A Survival Curriculum for Inner-City Kids" by KRS-One, September 9, 1989. Copyright © 1989 by The New York Times Company. Reprinted by permission.

The statistics used throughout are drawn from the following sources: *The State of Black America 1988* and *The State of Black America 1989*, both published by National Urban League, Inc. Reprinted by permission.

We are especially grateful to the photographers who gave permission to use their work: Peter Bodtke, Raymond Boyd, Glen E. Friedman, Ernie Paniccioli, and Ricky "Rickster" Powell retain copyright to their photographs. Thanks also to Jonathan Postal for the photographs which appear on pages 43, 51, and 66.

Acknowledgment is made to Magnum Press Images for use of the photos which appear on pages 21, 25, 62, and 64.

Book Design by Anne Scatto

Manufactured in the United States

First Edition

ACKNOWLEDGMENTS

To keep a very long story short, I just want to say a general thank-you to all the artists, record labels, video companies, and members of the Stop the Violence Movement who made all the "Self-Destruction" related projects work. Their names and individual contributions are recorded throughout the book.

For this book I specifically want to thank Duane Taylor of Jive Records, Leyla Turkkan and John Waller of Set To Run public relations, Terry Moorer of First Priority records, and Kevin Gibbs of the National Urban League. Pantheon Books editor David Sternbach proposed and believed in this project; Gerrie Summers utilized her position at *Word Up!* magazine to solicit the letters that are the heart of this effort; and John Jacob, President of the National Urban League, committed his organization to making this book available to its membership. Extra special enthusiasm and writing help came from Tracey Lewis, who did much of the grunt work. (What a way to spend a summer.) Mr. ED helped with his "editing for the '90s."

I want to thank the photographers who worked so hard to capture the spirit of the Movement on film, and who donated their work for this project. Ernie Paniccioli and Dorothy Low gave extra time and effort, and Dorothy provided transcripts from her video documentary *Stop the Violence: Rap Strikes Back*. Peter Bodtke, Raymond Boyd, Glen E. Friedman, Ernie Paniccioli, and Ricky "Rickster" Powell were all down with the project from the start, and their photos speak for themselves.

—*Nelson George*

We all agree tonight, all of the speakers have agreed that America has a very serious problem . . . Not only does America have a very serious problem, but our people have a very serious problem. America's problem is . . .

Chorus: Self-Destruction, ya headed for self-destruction. Self-Destruction, ya headed for self-destruction.

[repeat chorus 4 times]

Kris (KRS-One) Parker: Well, today's topic, self-destruction, it really ain't the rap audience that's buggin', it's one or two suckas, ignorant brothers, trying to rob and steal from one another. You get caught in the mid. So to crush that stereotype, here's what we did. We got ourselves together so that you can unite, and fight for what's right; not negative, 'cause the way we live is positive. We don't kill our relatives.

M.C. Delite: Pop, pop, pop, when it's shot who's to blame? Headlines, front page, and rap's the name. M.C. Delight here to state the bottom line: that Black-on-Black crime was way before our time.

Kool Moe Dee: Took a brother's life with a knife as his wife cried 'cause he died a trifling death. When he left his very last breath, was I slept, so watch your step. Back in the sixties our brothers and sisters were hanged. How could you gang bang? I never ever ran from the Ku Klux Klan and I shouldn't have to run from a Black man. Cause that's

[repeat chorus]

M.C. Lyte: Funky fresh, dressed to impress. Ready to party, money in your pocket. Dying to move your body, to get inside you pay the whole ten dollars scotch-taped with a razor blade to your collar. Leave the guns and the crack and the knives alone. M.C.

M.C. Lyte and DJ K-Rock shoot Lyte's section of "Self-Destruction."

Lyte's on the microphone. Bum rushin' and crushin', snatchin' and taxin', I cram to understand why brothers don't be maxin'. There's only one disco, they'll close one more. You ain't guardin' the door. So what you got a gun for? Do you rob the rich and give to the poor? Yo, Daddy-O, school 'em some more.

Daddy-O & Wise: Straight from the mouth of Wise and Daddy-O, do a crime end up in jail and gotta go 'cause you could do a crime and get paid today, and tomorrow you're behind bars in the worst way. Far from your family, 'cause you're locked away. Now tell me, do you really think crime pays? Scheming on taking what your brother has. You little suckers, you talkin' all that jazz.

D-Nice: It's time to stand together in a unity cause. If not, then yo, we're soon to be self-destroyed, unemployed, the rap race will be lost without a trace, or a clue, but what to do, is stop the violence and kick the science down the road that we call eternity, where knowledge is formed, and you'll learn to be self-sufficient, independent to teach to each is what rap intended, but society wants to invade. So do not walk this path that they laid. It's . . .

[*repeat chorus*]

Ms. Melodie: I'm Ms. Melodie and I'm a born-again rebel. The violence in rap must cease and settle if we want to develop and grow to another level. We can't be guinea pigs for the devil. The enemy knows that hip-hop rules, so we gotta get a grip and grab what's wrong. The opposition is weak and rap is strong.

Doug E. Fresh: This is all about, no doubt, to stop violence, but first let's have a moment of silence . . . swing . . . things been stated, re-educated, evaluated. Thoughts of the past have faded. The only thing left is the memories of our belated, and I hate it when someone dies and gets all hurt up for a silly gold chain by a chump. Word Up! It doesn't make you a big man and to want to go and dis your brother man, and you don't know that's part of the plan. Why? Cause rap music is in full demand, understand.

Just-Ice: My name is Just-Ice. A man, not a prankster. I was known as the gangster. But believe me, that is no fun. The time is now to unite everyone. You don't have to be soft to be for peace. Robbin' and killin' and murderin' is the least. You don't have to be chained by the beast. But, party-people, it time I release.

Heavy D: A-yo, here's the situation. Idiocy, nonsense, violence not a good policy. Therefore we must ignore fightin' and fussin'. Hev is at the door. So there'll be no bum-rushin'. Let's get together 'cause we're fallin' apart. I heard a brother shot another. It broke my heart, I don't understand the difficulty, people. Love your brother, treat him as an equal. They call us animals, mm . . . mm I don't agree with them. I'll prove them wrong, but right is what you're provin' them. Take heed before I lead to what I'm sayin' or we'll all be on our knees prayin'.

Fruit-Kwan: Yo, Heavy D, deep in the heart of the matter, the self-destruction is served on a platter. Making a day not failing to anticipate. They got greedy so they fell for the bait. That makes them a victim, picked then plucked new Jack in jail, but to the vets they're a duck. There's no one to rob, 'cause in jail you're a number. They never took the time to wonder about . . .

[*repeat chorus*]

Chuck D & Flavor Flav: Yes, we urge to merge we live for the love of our people the hope they get along, yeh! So we did a song, gettin' the point to our brothers and sisters, who don't know the time, boy! So we wrote a rhyme. It's dead in your head, you know, I'll drive to build and collect ourselves with intellect, come on. To revolve, to evolve to self-respect, 'cause we got to keep ourselves in check or else . . .

[*repeat chorus*]

Flavor Flav and the SW1's at the "Self-Destruction" video shoot.

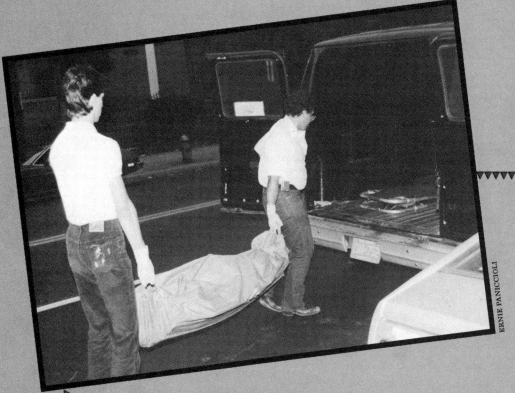

ERNIE PANICCIOLI

ERNIE PANICCIOLI

The price of self-destruction.

MAKING

SELF-DESTRUCTION

▲ ▼ ▲

On Saturday, September 10, 1987, the "Dope Jam" tour played Long Island's Nassau Coliseum. Kool Moe Dee, Boogie Down Productions, and Doug E. Fresh were among those on the bill. Kids from all over Long Island and the New York City area came anticipating great music and a good time.

Instead, for many it was a night of terror. Posses of black and Hispanic gangsters bought tickets with the intention of robbing and harassing innocent concertgoers. Security guards, when they could be found, did nothing to prevent the violence. Many people were stabbed, and one young man was murdered in a struggle over his gold chain. It was ugly, and rap music took all the blame.

Throughout that weekend, television and radio reporters joined newspaper headline writers in shouting "RAP VIOLENCE!" Rap and youth: evil and dangerous. The tragic episode was reported as if the music itself had inspired its young listeners to carve each other up. No one tried to understand the episode as a symptom, rather than a cause, of a violent society. They wanted to blame the kids. They wanted to blame rap.

These media attacks were not new. There have always been people who didn't like rap or the way its stars dressed, or who felt intimidated by its passionately committed, inner-city audience. The Nassau Coliseum violence gave these folks new ammunition. They didn't want to understand the music. They didn't write about protecting rap fans from young thugs. They didn't write about the responsibilities of the promoters or the security forces to prevent such occurrences. They didn't make distinctions between the gangsters and their victims, or acknowledge the strong positive messages of many rappers. Instead, they spread fear.

It was time for rappers to define the problem and defend themselves.

And they did.

The next Monday, September 12, phones all around New York began ringing. I called Ann Carli of Jive Records, and we recruited Jive's Chrissy Murray and Duane Taylor, First Priority's Terry Moorer, and Def Jam's Charlotte Hunter and Faith Newman. Leyla Turrkan, a publicist representing Public Enemy and Boogie Down Productions, immediately saw the need for some action. So did *Word Up!* magazine editor Gerrie Summers. It was this core of committed, young record-industry people who formed the backbone of the Stop the Violence Movement and who first met to discuss setting the record straight on rap.

The initial suggestion was that Boogie Down Productions' song entitled "Stop the Violence" be used as a theme for our group. Furthermore, I considered whether this song about crime at rap concerts and black-on-black crime might be the basis for an all-star rap record to raise public awareness, as "We Are the World" had done. From this idea others flowed: What about a music video? a concert? a protest rally? working for a black charity? What about making an entirely new record based on the "Stop the Violence" idea?

Over the course of the next year every one of these ideas would become a reality. Before going any further, though, we needed a name for our organization. "Stop the Violence" was the easy part. Some members opted for the "Stop the Violence Committee"; others preferred the name "Stop the Violence Group." But "Movement" was finally decided on because it suggests something that is progressing, that isn't exclusive, that is alive and growing.

We decided that the goals of the Stop the Violence Movement would be:

> **1.** for the rappers to raise public awareness of black-on-black crime and point out its real causes and social costs
>
> **2.** to raise funds for a charitable organization already dealing with the problems of illiteracy and crime in the inner city
>
> **3.** to show that rap music is a viable tool for stimulating reading and writing skills among inner-city kids.

Right from the beginning, certain rap stars were down with the Movement: KRS-One, D-Nice, Ms. Melodie, and other members of Boogie Down Productions' posse; the delightfully down Brooklyn rap-

Ms. Melodie, M.C. Lyte, and KRS-One perform "Self-Destruction" in concert.

per M.C. Lyte; black nationalist rappers Chuck D and Flavor Flav of Public Enemy, along with their producer, Hank Shocklee; Kool Moe Dee, who contributed insight as well as rapping; and the members of Stetsasonic, particularly Daddy-O and Delite.

As the drive intensified to make this still unnamed record, so did our efforts to recruit more rap stars. Some declined. Others said they were interested, but failed to come to our meetings. Los Angeles rap star Ice-T wanted to be involved, and would have given the record a bi-coastal feel, but when his *Power* album took off he was so busy that he couldn't make any of the STV recording sessions.

More encouraging was the surge of interest from other rappers once the word of our project spread. Heavy D was so enthusiastic that he had his manager, Andre Harrell, call both Ann Carli and me, and then he also called personally to ask about joining us. Just-Ice, a rapper with a violent image, was working on his second album with the help of KRS-One when he heard about STV. Some in the group felt he was too hard-core, but after much debate, and Just-Ice's pleading, he joined the crew.

Now we focused on the record itself. Hank Shocklee volunteered a track he had produced, and there was talk of using it. Then KRS-One arrived at an STV meeting with a track co-produced by D-Nice.

The track, "Self-Destruction," already featured KRS-One's scene-setting rap. We loved it, and decided that each rapper would write their own section, broken up into three to six line verses.

Each recording session was a little drama. No one ever showed up on time. Studio time was booked for 9 P.M. to 1 A.M., but people generally showed up at midnight and work really began at 1:30. At one session in Chinatown's Chun King Studio, everyone wondered if Kool Moe Dee would run into his rival L.L. Kool J, who was recording downstairs. And if he did, would L.L. agree to appear on the record? The answers were no and sort of, because although Moe Dee didn't show up, L.L. did. He didn't want to be on the record, but kept hanging around the studio. Soon M.C. Lyte arrived. She had written a rap based on statistics about black-on-black crime, but once in the studio she complained that it sounded too technical. She and L.L. talked about it and suddenly L.L. was kicking rhymes. He'd walk into our studio, rhyme with Lyte, go back downstairs, and then reappear with more suggestions. So, although he wasn't on the record, L.L. Kool J certainly contributed to it.

Later that night (much later) Doug E. Fresh arrived. He was down, but he had a complaint: the beat wasn't danceable enough. Since it was late, and folks were getting tired, the comment caused some tension. Together with Hank Shocklee, Fresh made a few suggestions for improving the track and turned his criticism into something positive. But Doug E. also used his distinctive "human beat box" sounds and back-up chants to create one of "Self-Destruction's" strongest moments.

At the main studio, Power Play, in Queens, STV sessions were held throughout October and November. Some nights the room was almost empty, as when Public Enemy's Chuck D and Flavor Flav laid down the vocals that closed "Self-Destruction." Other sessions were full-scale happenings, like the night Just-Ice, Heavy D, and four members of Stetsasonic laid their voices on the track. When the night began, Heavy D had his lines already prepared (as Kool Moe Dee had), but most of the other rappers came to the studio, listened to the music, and then wrote their rhymes. Stetsasonic's Fruit-Kwan, for example, sat silently in a chair for a long time before finally composing his memorable lines.

Throughout the hectic recording process, Carli, Hunter, and Jocelyn Cooper of Warner-Chappel Music worked hard to balance the artists' schedules with the studio time available. And after the vocals were finally captured on tape, D-Nice of Boogie Down Productions emerged as a key member of STV. He supervised the addition of sound effects, scratches, and samples that enriched "Self-Destruction." It was his idea to sweeten the track with bits of other records, so that Heavy D raps over a sample from his own "Overweight Lover"; and he added the echoes, reverb, and sounds of tape rewinding that help make the track sound so rich.

Originally we had planned to put the record out between Thanksgiving and Christmas of 1988. But at a meeting, we decided to release the record on January 15, Dr. Martin Luther King's birthday, making the record part of the celebration, and calling attention to the self-genocide that is threatening his legacy. This decision coincided with our choice of the National Urban League as the recipient of all funds raised by sales of "Self-Destruction." The Urban League is viewed by many as an old-fashioned civil rights organization, and we wondered whether they would want to be associated with rap. But the League's president, John Jacob, who is keenly aware of the problems facing black youth, wholeheartedly embraced STV. He assigned staff member Kevin Gibbs to help with the project, while executive vice president Frank Lomax III and vice president of development Donald Hense aided our efforts as well.

With the record completed and an organization selected as beneficiary, one other task remained: to raise money for a video. Jive had paid for the recording studio time, and RCA agreed to distribute "Self-Destruction" free of charge, but funds for the music video had to come from a variety of sources. The first $1,000 came from filmmaker Spike Lee. Pop-rock producer Nile Rodgers chipped in another $1,000, as did Wing Records president Ed Eckstine. Sylvia Rhone, vice president of Atlantic Records, which distributes Lyte and First Priority gave $5,000; Russell "Rush" Simmons, manager of Stetsasonic, provided $3,000. Other contributers who made the video possible were Uptown's Andre Harrell, WCI's Tom Draper, Tommy Boy's Tom Silverman and Monica Lynch, and Jive Records.

Chuck D and Just-Ice on 125th Street.

RICKY "RICKSTER" POWELL

PETER BODTKE

Director Lionel Martin (left) poses with members of the Classic Concepts crew and reporters covering the STV Movement.

The black-owned music video company Classic Concepts volunteered their services as well. Aside from making music videos, Classic Concepts' director Lionel "The Vid Kid" Martin and producer Ralph McDaniels run Video Music Box, a popular music video program on New York's Channel 31.

A number of different ideas were tossed around for the "Self-Destruction" video, and at one time it even looked as though it would be shot entirely within the walls of the New York City prison facility on Riker's Island. But conflicts with officials there made that impossible.

Instead, the video was shot at locations throughout Manhattan during one long, active weekend. We decided that a "master shot" featuring all the rappers should be intercut with scenes featuring smaller groups of rappers. So, bright and extra-early on the morning of Saturday, January 28, rappers, STV members, video makers, and fans gathered at Mount Morris Park for the exhausting but fun task of turning "Self-Destruction" into a hype video. Although musicians are not known for being early-risers, and some rap stars are notorious for being late to their own video shoots, on this winter morning those stereotypes were shattered. At the break of dawn, director Martin whisked Heavy D and Fruit-Kwan off to film their solo sections in front of a mural of Malcolm X in central Harlem.

Back at the park, a herd of television crews—including crews from MTV, Entertainment Tonight, and two European teams—gathered, along with reporters and photographers, to record this historic event. Producer and writer Mtume, who was a political activist before starting his musical career, brought his old wisdom to bear as he conducted a series of interviews. His presence was an indictment of all the music industry veterans who dislike rap and yet would never volunteer for a black self-help project such as this one. Some other artists who participated, like Oran "Juice" Jones, maker of the hit "The Rain," had a personal stake in the Movement. His younger brother Dean had been stabbed repeatedly at the violent Nassau Coliseum show and had to be hospitalized. (Dean tells his story on page 23.)

By noon everyone had climbed to the peak of Mount Morris Parkway, with its panoramic view of Harlem, and prepared for the group shots that appear throughout the video. During the wait, Flavor Flav entertained the crowd with jokes that had them roaring. Nevertheless, Public Enemy caused a minor crisis when lead rapper Chuck D, who had been in the studio the night before, failed to show up. How much this would effect the editing of the video we weren't sure, but we knew it would be a problem. On the positive side, Tone Loc—maker of the phenomenal hit single "Wild Thing"—and another Los Angeles rapper, Young M.C., flew in to be down with the Movement. Despite the cold weather, the video shoot turned into a giant party, with rappers dancing and Kool Moe Dee and Flavor Flav getting busy for the crowd. Things were going superbly, but there was much more to do.

A few blocks from New York's City Hall is a big, gray, foreboding courthouse called The Tombs. The scenes with Tone Loc and Young M.C., Stetsasonic's Daddy-O and Delite, and Just-Ice were filmed there in a hot, green-and-gray-walled holding cell. Being in prison, even for a few hours, was a disheartening experience for all involved, and knowing that so many young black men (*and* women) spend years of their lives behind bars made us even more committed in our efforts.

Sunday morning the walls of the world famous Schomburg Library for Research in Black Culture echoed with the sound of "Self-Destruction." This building, which contains one of the world's largest collections of books and periodicals on African-American life, was the setting for the hip-hop roundtable that opens the video. I made my most visible contribution to the video in this scene, by suggesting that a postcard of the STV logo be placed on the book that KRS-One holds in the opening shot.

After spending most of the day at Schomburg, we traveled to a cemetery in upper Manhattan to "steal" a shot. Without having permission to be there, the crew, along with Doug E. Fresh, the Awesome Two, Red Alert, and Marley Marl, entered the lot and stood in front of an open grave to symbolize the ravages of crime. Fresh, perhaps the best performer in hip-hop, gave a typically charismatic performance in this scene.

The final location was the boarded-up entrance to the Latin Quarter, once the city's top rap nightspot, and now itself a victim of black-on-black crime. Outbreaks of mugging and chain-snatching had forced it to close. This was the only "Self-Destruction" location in midtown Manhattan, and the cameras attracted a large crowd. M.C. Lyte was there to film her section, and so was Big Daddy Kane, who shot a cameo surrounded by girls recruited from the crowd.

By the time we had finished shooting the video, the record had been selling out of record stores for four weeks. At noon on the day of its release, over fifty radio stations played the song, and spoke of its significance in relation to black culture, and the upcoming Black History Month. In order not to lose the momentum we had gained with the record, we would have to edit and complete the video as soon as possible. The Urban League supplied the statistics that ran at the bottom of the frame. Classic Concepts worked on the opening and closing graphics for the clip. The rough footage looked great, but one problem remained: Chuck D's absence. We solved part of this problem by scheduling time for Chuck and spinner Terminator X to be filmed at their college radio station, Adelphi's WBAU. But the other problem was that we were now almost out of money, and couldn't afford to shoot this section in film. Instead, we had to use videotape, but thanks to some creative lighting and editing by Martin, only the truly discerning can tell the difference.

With Ann Carli and Chrissy Murray mobilizing Jive's staff, and with the cooperation of RCA, the video and record became the most important 12-inch single of early 1988. Still, there was much more to be done. At the urging of publicist Leyla Turkkan, a march through Harlem was organized. Movement members decided that on February 14, we would walk with a coffin from the Apollo Theater to the Adam Clayton Powell State Office Building together with a group of high school students. Once inside the State Office Building, a press conference would be held and the "Self-Destruction" video debuted. And that's what happened—but it was not quite so cut-and-dried.

I helped carry the coffin, along with Fab Five Freddy of "Yo, MTV Raps," Chuck D, Daddy-O, Delite, KRS-One, and Just-Ice. As we moved through the throng of press, police, and students, I felt I was in the Harlem of twenty years ago, when demonstrations like this were common. The coffin was heavy, and the walk only a few hundred yards, but it seemed to take an hour. At the doors to the State Office Building, Chuck and Daddy-O grabbed microphones and spoke to the crowd.

Upstairs, the gallery was jammed with press and young people, predominantly adolescents and teens. The words spoken by the rappers and the teens, which you can read in this book, convey the pride and passion of that day and, truly, of this entire project.

■ ■ ■

PETER BODTKE

RICKY "RICKSTER" POWELL

The video crew sets up the final shot for "Self-Destruction." ▲

Nelson George at the Harlem rally organized by Stop the Violence members. ▶

Since the Harlem march, "Self-Destruction" has sold half a million copies and generated over $200,000 for the community programs of the Urban League. The Movement has also become part of a great trend toward the ideas of black pride and brotherhood among youth. It has always been my contention that music, used purposefully, can be a powerful tool for social change, and the making of "Self-Destruction" and its impact have provided some of the proudest moments of my life.

The Stop the Violence Movement has shown that rap, because it speaks to and for young black America, can help reach the most alienated members of our community and boost the confidence of young people who are striving, against the most severe economic and social obstacles, to do the right thing.

Nelson George

CRIME

D. Nice. ▲

Doug E. Fresh and
Heavy D relax at the ▶
video shoot.

Is NOT a Part of Our Black Heritage

© LEONARD FREED/MAGNUM PHOTOS

There are many people in America who believe that our country's youth are irresponsible, our country's youth have no conscience, our country's youth lack motivation, invention, direction. The young people of the Stop the Violence Movement contradict these notions. The truth is, these young people *refuse* to accept them. These young people have united, bonded by common cause, to communicate the idea that crime is not acceptable in African-American communities.

We all know the statistics and have been victimized (directly or indirectly) by crime. When compared to white Americans, it is a fact that:

- African-Americans are *twice* as likely to be victims of violent crimes and are *twice* as likely to be robbed
- 90 percent of robberies against blacks are committed by other blacks
- 85 percent of the assaults in the black community are cases of blacks assaulting blacks
- 95 percent of all homicides committed by blacks are against other blacks
- for African-American males, ages 16 to 34, murder is the leading cause of death.

Quite simply, if you think black-on-black crime isn't your problem, we say you should think again. In the six minutes that it takes these rap artists on the song to express their collective disdain for black-on-black crime, two African-Americans will have become victims. So, if you have not already been victimized, chances are you or someone very close to you will. These statistics, however, are not part of what we call our African-American heritage.

Violence seems to be so much a part of modern culture, but robbing and stealing and killing one another are unacceptable destroyers of our communities. The National Urban League and the People of the Stop the Violence Movement believe community is just another word for "family."

We hope to re-emphasize this ideal for some, and introduce it to others.

The money generated by the Stop the Violence Movement will go to support existing programs designed to combat black-on-black crime, to help develop new programs in areas where crime is most prevalent, and to our national Education Initiative—all of which, we believe, are key to raising the consciousness and levels of responsible behavior among our young people.

We understand that there is no quick fix to the ills of criminal behavior. No single record or humanitarian gesture can wipe crime from our streets . . . or prevent someone bent on destruction from robbing, stealing, or killing in his or her neighborhood. What we *do* believe is that attitudes can and must change.

Attitudes must change about how we view crime—that is, we must learn *and teach* that criminal behavior is not acceptable. Attitudes must change about how we deal with criminals: we must assume responsibility for the destructive activity that affects our communities, taking social control by cooperating with those responsible for enforcing the laws. In fact, we must *demand* that we, who are disproportionately affected by crime, be given the attention and protection necessary to help deter criminal activity. Finally, and most importantly, attitudes must change about the way we perceive ourselves, both individually and collectively. African-Americans must demonstrate respect for themselves as well as others in their community. Self-respect breeds responsible behavior.

The "Self-Destruction" record and video and the other messages of the Stop the Violence Movement represent a conscious step in the right direction. We at the National Urban League applaud the efforts of these young artists as they help us to reach other young people with the message, "Crime is not part of our black heritage."

Statement by Frank Lomax III,
Executive Vice-President
of the National Urban League
February 14, 1989

NASSAU COLISEUM

SEPTEMBER 10, 1987

Everything was dark, all you could see was the stage. I was in the aisle, a security guard was about fifty yards away. The next thing I know, there are like twenty people in the aisle but nothing had happened yet. This guy saw me with my gold so he reached for my bracelet because my hand was on the railing. Then I grabbed him. Once I grabbed him the whole crowd rushed behind me and I turned around to see the crowd and there were bodies flying. So I ducked down, and when I did, people just piled on top of me. I didn't realize I was stabbed until everything was all over. By this time, all my chains, gold watch, and bracelet were gone. A friend of mine was hit in the head because he was trying to help me out. Then the security guard comes over and starts asking questions. But at this point, I didn't want to hear anything from him, I wanted to find out what had happened. It wasn't until my friend told me that I had blood all over my pants that I turned around and lifted up my shirt and all of this blood starts gushing out. So I went to the first-aid office, but the office was crowded, full of people who had been stabbed or cut. So there had to be some kind of SWAT team going around stabbing and cutting people up. It was crazy.

It probably wouldn't have made a difference if the security guard had come over, they probably would have taken him out too. Security couldn't have been that strong if they (criminals) were going through the whole Coliseum. The whole area was affected; one kid was killed.

No matter how poor you are, why would you try to kill people to take what they have? If they had rolled on me, I would've given it to them. What was I going to do, there were twenty of them and one of me. But they figured that he's not going to do that, so let's snuff him out . . . and take his gold. If they have that kind of mentality, that they don't think my life is worth anything, what could their lives be worth? Nothing. It's just crazy. It doesn't make any sense that they would kill someone over something like gold—gold that they're going to sell to buy drugs.

Dean Jones

The letters excerpted here and throughout the book, were written by young people from around the country in response to a Stop the Violence essay contest sponsored by *Word Up!* magazine. Readers from ages twelve to eighteen were asked to talk about their experiences with black-on-black crime, the impact of drugs in their communities, the fashion of wearing gold chains and jewelry, the role of rap music in their lives, and anything else they felt was pertinent. The result was a tall stack of letters that describe vividly the ways young blacks and others live today. They have almost all been hurt, directly or indirectly, by violence or drugs, but they also have hope and determination to improve their communities. They are angry that rap music has taken the blame for a larger social problem, but they don't hesitate to criticize rappers who boast about guns and money. And they see the Stop the Violence Movement as a model for people who want to take a stand.

My mother's boyfriend got robbed one night. This wasn't fair, a black man getting robbed by someone just like him. Just because he wanted something from my mother's boyfriend that he didn't have. It's just like KRS said in "Self-Destruction": "It's one or two suckas / ignorant brothers / trying to rob and steal from one another."

Keisha W., age 13
Albany, New York

I have been in many fights where I have been stabbed over a pair of Troops or a Troop jumpsuit. I didn't realize the danger my life was in until my brother was shot. I realized who my real friends were; the ones who told me to keep selling while my brother was in the hospital were the ones who wanted to hang around me just because I had money.

I decided to stop selling because I didn't want to get shot like my brother. Everybody was calling me weak, but I didn't care. Most of the time kids like to wear all of the expensive clothes and jewelry to let everybody know that they have money. But most of the time, the people who wear and buy all of that stuff have the least time to enjoy it.

Tracee H., age 15
Houston, Texas

I would like to approach the problem like this: black-on-black crime starts with the mistreatment of blacks by whites because of their skin color. I know a couple of ways to stop violence. With more funds to provide better housing and chances for successful jobs, violence could be decreased. I am a white male who grew up in the projects for 14 years. Black-on-black crime must stop.

Jason R., age 18
Raleigh, North Carolina

EUGENE RICHARDS/MAGNUM PHOTOS

Once, when I was going to West Philly High for summer school I witnessed a terrible crime. A girl was punched in the face when she refused to give up her gold jewelry and Gucci bag. Two black men walked on either side of her, deliberately tripping her while checking out her gold. I was across the street and I was walking so fast you could say I was running. Some guys from school saw what was going on and rushed in to help, but the two guys still got away with her stuff.

Renee G., age 16
Philadelphia, Pennsylvania

Once the Fort Greene projects used to be a peaceful neighborhood. People would stay outside and talk, play their radios, kids would play with their friends and just hang out. Then a new addictive drug called crack appeared. The people changed, the playground has become a battlefield for rival crackheads and crack dealers. Crackheads are all over the projects. Fort Greene is now nothing more than a time bomb just waiting to explode. No one is safe. Now there are muggings, murders, and robberies. There is not one day when a crack dealer doesn't get busted and in a few days he's set free. This is an endless cycle . . .

The communities are slowly becoming our deathtraps. They are becoming prey to drug lords and gangs.

Shawika S., age 16
Brooklyn, New York

The black-on-black crime I experienced was over a silly matter. Luckily, I didn't get hurt because the crime didn't happen to me. It was just a matter of being at the wrong place at the wrong time. After lifting weights, my four friends and I headed to the store to get some orange juice. As we walked, we came upon three guys who were trying to "bogart" the sidewalk. I politely said excuse me, but one of my friends exchanged a few words with one of the guys who blocked the sidewalk. Before I knew it, one of the guys pulled a gun. My friends and I ran. My best friend Eric was shot in the wrist. Things like that hurt me and the community severely. The way I feel about the situation is that if a person must use a gun to settle a petty dispute like the situation I experienced, then whoever is in charge of military usage and guns should put a lock on the weapons chest forever.

Andre F., age 17
Detroit, Michigan

What is music? Music is a form of expressing ideas with musical tones and lyrics. Anyone can listen to and enjoy music. Everyone has their own musical tastes. Not everyone from Tennessee likes country music and not everyone from Boston likes classical music. People form their own opinions according to what they like and dislike and go on from there.

Jevonda G., age 17
Louisville, Kentucky

In my school I always hear white people saying, "Man, that 'Self-Destruction' video makes no sense." They are dead wrong, because everything that is said in the song is so true, so strong and so powerful!

Rashidah B., age 13
Springfield, New Jersey

Rap music is not what makes people commit violent crimes. It is the people themselves and the way they were brought up that makes them. Rap music and concerts should be enjoyed by all who attend, and people should not be afraid to go.

Kellee H., age 18
Louisville, Kentucky

I am 13 years old and I have never been to a rap concert or any concert for that matter. The reason is violence at the concerts.

Gold chains do not invite crime, but people who want them and let greed overcome them do . . .

First of all, rap is a great new way to communicate with today's children because they understand information better when it's in rap form. Rap music expresses how a rapper feels, and helps people who listen to it see how life is through his eyes.

Latiesha J., age 13
Brooklyn, New York

I really don't have much experience with black-on-black crime, but I do know a number of people involved in it and I know what is going on in the world of crime today.

We just recently got a bad reputation. A number of people were arrested for dealing (one was caught so far, but there are two the police don't know about), murders (three arrested), rape (the man wasn't reported to police), and countless robberies. My friends are barely allowed to come to my house anymore because of all this violence here and it's not only adults. It's kids ranging in age from 14 to 19. The amount of violence is growing larger everyday.

Christina G., age 13
Piermont, New York

The image some rappers portray, is sometimes very violent—such as Easy E, Dre, and Yella of the Compton, California rap group NWA. The group raps about being in jail, which gives the impression of being a joke. They also rap about drinking and using drugs in their singles "Straight Outta Compton" and "Gangsta Gangsta." NWA also sings of violent acts such as beating or shooting people. These songs make it look like it's cool to go out and kill someone.

Corey J., age 17
Louisville, Kentucky

A WORD ON RAP

Tone Loc and Afrika Bambaataa in Mount Morris Park.

L et me let you in on a secret. When I first started editing *Word Up!* magazine, I was not a rap music fan. I had my favorite message-oriented tracks—like Grandmaster Flash, and the Furious Five's "The Message," and "White Lines" with Melle Mel—but I was really expecting this "fad" to end. In fact, like most of rap's detractors, I had little understanding of the music. I thought of it as monotonous, obnoxious noise, and I seldom listened to what the artists were saying. Furthermore, as rap was coming up, I was on the staff of a rather shallow fanzine whose concept of popular black youth music centered on Michael Jackson, Prince, and New Edition. No one seemed to care about the music black youth was making for themselves.

But as I became interested in what teens were saying and doing, I had the chance to help launch a new magazine where I would be responsible for both the features and the overall focus. In creating a magazine for black teens, I had to cover what black teens wanted. They wanted rap. But they also wanted something more than just cute pin-ups of New Edition. They wanted articles and interviews that spoke to them about *them*. They wanted insights into the complexities of life. They wanted something that told them they were special, in a society that tells them there is an American dream yet forces them to experience nightmares. And they wanted to know about things that could be attained through work, faith, education, and sound goals. For them, the world of rap music is where it all came together.

For many reasons, black youth—the nation's youth—are experiencing an enormous amount of pain and confusion. With parents often either preoccupied or absent, unable or unwilling to communicate with them sufficiently, they need someone to look up to. Often it is a high-profile figure, either a sports star or a recording artist, and in the 1980s the recording star is often a rapper.

I think *Word Up!* has been successful not only because it profiles the rappers the youth often look up to and emulate, but because it tries to speak the truth and accepts its readers as conscious young adults. We listen to their views and don't cover up our eyes—or theirs—in the face of issues.

I have to admit, however, that I have often felt turmoil inside because of many rap artists. In reading about their imprudent antics, I was dismayed that I was promoting artists who shirked the responsibilities entertainers should gain along with their success. While some had positive images, it seemed that twice as many had destructive images promoting crime, thoughtless sexual behavior, and an unmanly machismo. But if I censored all the rappers whose views I disagreed with or detested, *Word Up!* would not exist. As an editor, I could only present all sides of the rap scene, showing the benefits of the positive and the self-destructiveness of the negative. As it turned out, though, both the rappers and the fans were already thinking for themselves.

The Stop the Violence Movement came along at the right time. Rappers, like everyone else, have to pay attention to, and be responsible for, their actions. Now, the artists in the Movement are raising questions about how many teens sport gold chains, about concert security, about social responsibility in general. "It's important for the rap audience to start carrying itself in a more respectable manner," KRS-One told me, speaking from the studio in which one of the "Self-Destruction" sessions was taking place. "All the other music industries have violence and riots. Rap is the only one with the spotlight on it. So we should show peace and some kind of harmony within our industry and in our concepts and our concerts." Rappers also have to think about whether they are really exercising the first amendment when they make outrageous statements or merely amending their raps to make a profit off of potential record buyers.

It is true that teenagers are much smarter than we think. That is exactly why we should give them proper lessons. We have a long way to go to stop the violence in our community. One song can't do it alone, says Kris, but, "What ['Self-Destruction'] will do is give listeners an alternative to the everyday music they normally listen to that is just [encouraging] them to do violence," he continues. "And it's those records that the rap industry has to say it's now time to cease. It's like a power move among artists to finally declare, once and for all, that the violence in our community is destroying us—it's 'Self-Destruction.'"

On my way to a meeting about this book, there was a group of young students on the train en route to or from a school outing. I listened as a young child—he couldn't have been more than eight or nine—recite, word for word, the lyrics to "Self-Destruction." I was impressed and enheartened. Then I watched him walk up to one of the adult chaperones and comment on his leather medallion. No, it did not have at its center the motherland of Africa or the face of Malcolm X or any other symbol of African-American pride. In the center of the glistening black cowhide was a bullet. It seemed that even the child, after reciting those words against violence, found this symbol very strange. Clearly it will take a lot more than speaking to the youth about violence to end violence when adults so casually perpetuate this evil.

When I sat down at my computer to write this, thinking about how difficult this Movement would be, I overheard Arsenio Hall doing his monologue and mentioning a major rap concert on the West Coast over the Fourth of July weekend. Two men in the audience, he's saying, broke into a fight at the concert, and I think: That's just all I need. But as they were fighting, all of a sudden sixty thousand fans started chanting the words "Self-destruction! You're heading for self-destruction!" Apparently the two brawlers stopped, and as they looked into the crowd, they felt very stupid. Now, I can honestly say, I *am* a fan of rap music.

Gerrie Summers

KRS-ONE
BOOGIE DOWN PRODUCTIONS

Basically, this began three years ago, when a riot broke out after a show we did. We went home that night and wrote this song called "Stop the Violence." When I say we, I mean me and Scott LaRock. It was supposed to be on the album *Criminal Minded*, but because of the way people perceived recording artists, we waited. So when the second album, *By Any Means Necessary*, came out, we put it on that album.

That record is basically about club violence and national violence. The problem is to deal specifically with black-on-black violence. "Self-Destruction" is part two, the second step in that campaign.

The record was put together by Ann Carli, Nelson George, and myself. My production team produced it and I mixed it. We're not trying to front, we're not just telling the kids, "We made a record about stopping the violence, so just stop the violence!" Nonsense. We're telling everyone—the police officers and the industry—that there is a more serious side to rap music.

When Ann Carli of Jive and Nelson George of *Billboard* approached me about making a "Stop the Violence" part two, I realized that there are so many rappers around—"You might as well get a little more creative, a little more original." The project was handed down to D-Nice to produce the track while everyone else wrote their own lyrics.

Scott would have been all for it, being the co-creator of "Stop the Violence." What most people don't know is that Scott co-wrote it with me, but we just didn't get a chance to put it out because the industry wanted rap artists to say "Yo man" and all that other sh—. Rap artists saying "Stop the Violence" wasn't the appropriate thing at the time, so we had to wait. Scott left us—died—before the second album came out, and I had to put it out myself. (See Scott LaRock's story, page 47.)

World peace is the issue. I want to be remembered as the first ghetto kid to jump up for world peace, because the stereotype is that all ghetto kids want to do is sell drugs and rob each other, which isn't fact. I came from the heart of the ghetto—there ain't no suburbia in me!

The reality of life is, you have to survive, one way or another. On top of that, you have to stay intelligent. So you surround yourself with knowledge and these things are like milestones in your life, if you know where you're going.

DADDY-O
STETSASONIC

I have been at concerts, when we were in Santa Monica on the Public Enemy tour, where the gangs broke out—oh, my god, I never saw nothing like that! People don't even think when they start fighting, they just fight.

A lot of parents, especially black parents, don't realize that they have a hand in creating these monsters. Elijah Muhammad said that you can't change a people until you change their way of thinking.

Stetsasonic feels that one of the primary duties of a rap artist in this day and age is to become a positive role model in the minds and the hearts of children. These kids don't have positive role models to look up to. In most neighborhoods, drug dealers are the role models. So, I hope we can continue to do projects like this and show them something to look forward to, and hopefully the parents can become better role models in the home, too. A lot of what we experience—black-on-black crime, drugs in the neighborhood—is because we don't have role models in the home, heroes in the home. So the drug dealer becomes the hero. Society tells us to get a big car and house and you've made it. So the kid drops out of school and makes $3,000 a week! If we can continue to show better ways to do it and be better role models than the ones they see on the street, then I think a lot of what we're trying to do will be established.

Stop the Violence executive directors Ann Carli and Nelson George. ▲

Gathered for the final shot of "Self-Destruction" are (left to right) Teddy Ted, Delite, Kool Moe Dee, Tone Loc, and Daddy-O. ▶

Ms. Melodie at the "Self-Destruction" video shoot. ▼

PETER BODTKE

Heavy D and Classic Concepts director Lionel Martin
▲ *rehearse D's scene in front of a mural of Malcolm X in Harlem. Gee Whiz of the Boyz walks in the background.*

Stetsasonic's Delite and Bobby Simmons, accompanied
▼ *by two friends, prepare to perform the chorus of "Self-Destruction."*

PETER BODTKE

An assistant on the Classic Concepts film crew holds the clapboard before shooting a ▶ scene in the Schomburg Library in Harlem.

Cinematographer Larry Banks sets up the opening shot of the ▼ "Self-Destruction" video.

▲ *KRS-One is interviewed by journalist Ben Mapp.*

◀ *Kool Moe Dee, Flavor Flav, and Afrika Bambaataa.*

When Nelson George and Tokyo Rose (Ann Carli) let us know they were putting together a record to try to cut down the violence in the USA and abroad, we were down with that because it was something that was in our hearts.

The part I rap about is about being in jail. A lot of times people in our community don't know what it's like to be on the inside. I know, and it's not a very pretty picture. They don't understand what it means to be locked away, to be far from your family and be controlled every morning and have a scheduled wake-up, etc. Not to mention that a lot of crime goes on in jail—anything from getting shanked with a toothbrush to getting raped. Kids committing crime don't think about these things. So what I speak about is the inside: "You could do a crime and get paid today, and tomorrow you're behind bars in the worst way. / Far from your family, 'cause you're locked away. Now tell me, do you really think crime pays?"

KOOL MOE DEE

The media always blows up and tries to connect rap music to the violence. Something has to be done—or at least addressed by the media, in our view—so that people can get a better perspective on what's going on. The violence is not caused by the rap fans. It's caused by bandits who come to the rap shows to prey on young kids who are there to enjoy the show.

You go to a Bruce Springsteen concert and you don't see any white boys killing each other. But in a rap show where the audience is predominantly black, you see black-on-black crime. It's like a sickness that no one is really paying attention to.

Rap artists are into something besides making money. It's at the point where we're trying to show that we really care about the fans, and not just the fans but the black community, because that's where rap music is generated from, and for. We think that because we have this spotlight and the attention of youth we can utilize this to become young black leaders, so to speak, since they don't have real positive images to identify with. So I think doing things like this [STV] and talking about something relevant—I'm not saying that every record is going to be about Stop the Violence, but we *are* going to acknowledge and address that it's a problem—shows a certain amount of responsibility that might influence a lot of people to get serious and look at themselves in a different way. I think it has to do with your frame of mind and how you're thinking. Like, the guys who are robbing and stealing aren't looking at it as a black-on-black thing, they're just going for theirs and not looking at what they're doing to the race as a whole!

FLAVOR FLAV

PUBLIC ENEMY

We are role models. We have to do the right thing in front of them, say the right thing in front of them, at all times. We have to try and teach them to strive for perfection because that is the right direction and if anything is wrong we will make a correction. And we will do that because we have methods of detection.

What goes around comes around—and, man, God don't like ugly. The way you live is the way you get treated.

D-NICE

I feel that black-on-black crime is really ignorant, because they're not robbing each other over anything worthwhile. It's over stupid gold chains. If kids stopping wearing the chains then they wouldn't have anything to get robbed of.

M.C. DELITE

STETSASONIC

Black-on-black crime started way before rap music even began. We try to be informative and let the people know it's not the music but the people themselves—it's a failure of communication, of education, a failure of the school system, and the parents. We know that the parents are the bridge to the future, and that the children *are* the future. So because of lack of education and lack of moral respect for one another you have violence. Now they think it's okay to steal a gold chain, take money, and stuff like that. It's so ridiculous in this day and time that our own brothers and sisters have to pick up arms against one another.

In black-on-black crime, we only hurt ourselves, we make ourselves look like fools. If you want to take over something, you want to pick something up, pick one of those abandoned buildings and try to build something out of that. It's all about building. If you want to have something, you don't want something petty from someone's neck, you want a building, you want to be an entrepreneur. Something more positive. All that other stuff is weak.

FRUIT-KWAN

STETSASONIC

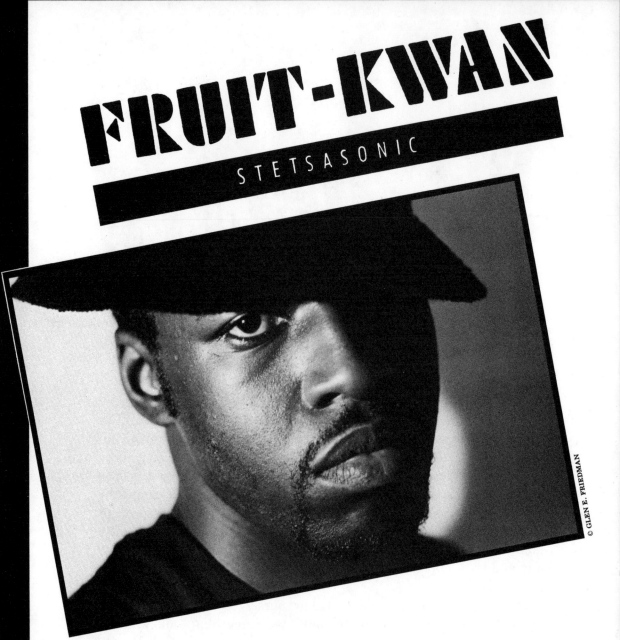

© GLEN E. FRIEDMAN

The more events there are like this, the more successful the understanding will be toward the black population and culture.

HEAVY D

© GLEN E. FRIEDMAN

One of the main reasons we got involved with this project is because we strongly believe violence is nonsense, and that we've got to get together as one. Looking around, I see a whole lot of rappers coming together.

You pay your money to see a show but you end up seeing a boxing match. It's disgusting. People get scared to go places, you can't sit around and do anything without somebody trying to threaten your life.

JUST-ICE

© GLEN E. FRIEDMAN

Our music is a form of communication. If we can understand the situation, then maybe you'll understand.

You want to perform. You come in with a good attitude, but you can't do your work. It used to be that everyone knew each other. Now people come from all over—Bronx, Queens—with all of this borough conflict. It just causes trouble!

STATISTICS

In 1986, blacks comprised approximately 12 percent of the U.S. population. Yet during that year, blacks accounted for 27 percent of all arrests reported to the FBI, 46.5 percent of all arrests for violent crimes, and 30.2 percent of all arrests for property crimes. Of all murder arrests in 1986, blacks accounted for 48 percent of the total. That same year, blacks accounted for 46.6 percent of all rape arrests, 62 percent for robberies, 39.8 percent for assault, 29.5 percent for burglary, 30.1 percent for theft, and 34.7 percent for auto theft. In respect to city arrests, blacks accounted for 30.8 percent of the total arrests made in 1986.

The leading cause of death among black males between the ages of 15 and 24 is homicide. Approximately 42 per 100,000 blacks between the ages of 15 and 24 die from homicide. This compares with about 8 per 100,000 whites in the same age group.

Black men comprise only 6 percent of the U.S. population but make up almost 50 percent of the prisoners in local, state, and federal jails.

More than 18 percent of black males drop out of high school.

A 1989 survey by the New York State Division of Criminal Justice said that the profile of that state's most likely murder victim was a 27-year-old African-American male shot with a hand gun in a drug-related dispute. In eighty-two percent of the murders, blacks killed other blacks. Ninety-five percent of the time the killers were men whose average age was 22. So in New York we see a terrifying pattern of young African-American men shooting their elders in a fight over drugs.

It is this unholy alliance of guns and drugs that is perpetrating self-destruction among African-Americans.

THE BLACK-ON-BLACK CRIME STATE OF MIND

"I never ever ran from the Ku Klux Klan and I shouldn't have to run from a black man."

—*Kool Moe Dee, from "Self-Destruction"*

A black man hangs by his neck from a tree like a puppet on a string. Below him, a crowd of whites are gathered, celebrating his murder. Many of them hold torches that illuminate not only the darkness, but the brutality America once practiced against its brown-skinned citizens. The victim, a black man accused of a crime, has been denied trial by jury. Instead, this man, like too many of his peers, was presumed guilty by virtue of his skin color. It is a sad truth that for much of this century the lynching of blacks, primarily black males of all ages, was a problem that haunted the lives of African-Americans every day.

Tuskegee Institute, the black university founded in Alabama by Booker T. Washington, did a survey of lynchings from 1900 to 1919. Tuskegee reported 115 lynchings in 1900, 130 in 1901, 99 in 1903, 97 in 1908, 69 in 1915 and 83 in 1919. In only one year of the survey were there fewer than 50 lynchings (38 in 1917). Keep in mind that not all lynchings were reported to law enforcement or the press, so these were just estimates.

Lead by groups like the Ku Klux Klan, these murders were the physical expression of a philosophy of white supremacy that dominated the south and, to a lesser degree, the rest of the United States. Through what were called Jim Crow laws, blacks were excluded from the mainstream of national life. The freedoms blacks now take for granted were denied them just a few decades ago. Lynchings and KKK threats planted fear in the minds of many.

Yet, African America survived. Despite restrictive laws and violence, the sons and daughters of slaves pushed forward. In the courts and on the streets, blacks overturned Jim Crow and diminished this nation's acceptance of racism. From the end of World War II until the early 1970s, the barriers that denied equal opportunity were attacked and often shattered. That doesn't

At the Urban League conference, Delite makes a point.

mean racism disappeared. No way. It does mean that evil acts like lynchings have stopped. But current roadblocks to advancement often take the form of institutional racism—prejudice disguised by seemingly reasonable rules and regulations.

The era of lynch mobs may be history, but in the 1990s black Americans are still not safe in their own homes. A new kind of terror grips black neighborhoods. it is the drug-related violence that is killing blacks in ever increasing numbers. Drugs have had a disastrous impact on black life ever since heroin first became popular. Then came PCP (or "Angel Dust"), cocaine, and now the most addictive substance of all, crack. Crack has corrupted the will of its victims. It has transformed working-class communities into battlefields where drug-dealing replaces hope. The battle for civil rights, once at the top of the black agenda, has been replaced by a full-scale war on drugs and the death-peddlers who sell them.

Police brutality, to many the contemporary equivalent of lynching, is still a problem; but an even more ominous problem is how to stem the tide of self-genocide created by drug use. Junkies rob, and often kill, to support their habit. Dealers murder customers and each other over money. Crack destroys everything it touches. It respects no sex or class boundaries. Any way you look at it, drugs are self-destruction.

In recent years, rap music has been tagged as a source of black-on-black violence. Its critics deplore the language of rap and the criminal acts that have marred so many concerts. One of raps greatest strengths is its emphasis on day-to-day reality. Unlike R&B and pop music, rap depicts the life of its audience and stars with honesty. If, for example, you placed five current rap hits in a time capsule and opened it up in the year 2090, you'd get a very detailed picture of black life in the 1990s. The future listener would know about the slang, clothes, cars, and attitudes toward sex, racism, and violence many of us have today. In contrast to the blandness of pop, rap tells true stories in everyday language. If its subjects and styles offend, it may be that rap is simply too real for narrow minds.

The problem of violence at rap concerts can be addressed with equal directness, because it is no different than black-on-black crime in general. There are young criminals among African-Americans who make a living preying on their brothers and sisters. Often motivated by drug use, they rob and steal from people in their own community. At rap concerts, where they blend in easily with young concertgoers, these criminals do their dirty business just as they would anywhere else.

The problem isn't rap music. The problem lies in the impact of poverty, unemployment, and drugs—especially crack—on young people. Which is why Kool Moe Dee's line about the Ku Klux Klan from "Self-Destruction" is so powerful. In linking the oppression of the past with the violence of today, the rap star suggests that black people must show again today the commitment and unity against adversity that they have shown in the past.

Nelson George

45

The Stop the Violence Movement in full effect.

Father. Son. Friend. DJ. Rapper. Idol. Black. Dead. Statistic.

Those staccato words give us only a glimpse of one who briefly rose above the preordained life of a young black man from the inner city.

To most of the world, Scott "LaRock" Sterling was invisible. He didn't exist outside of the insular, black, hip-hop world. As a child, Scott would rush to Cedar Park in the Bronx on his purple bike to hear DJ Kool Herc jam in the dark, until his mother would call him home for an old-fashioned butt-whipping. Mom didn't want her child involved in the music business.

So Scott channeled some of his energy into becoming the neighborhood basketball star, earning the nickname "LaRock." LaRock was a player who "rocked" the game with his high scoring. But unlike many of his urban companions, Scott wasn't going to end up shooting ball in an unkempt playground for the rest of his life. He followed his mother's wishes and, in 1984, graduated from Castleton State College in Vermont with a degree in business administration.

Fresh out of college, Scott found a job as a social worker at the Franklin Armory Men's Shelter in the Bronx. Scott wasn't like some blacks who earned a degree and broke the hell out. He came back, back home to the people he knew needed him.

Kris Parker was already well versed in the ways of the street by the time he reached the Armory by a different path in 1984. He had spent the last seven of his twenty short years on the street. He was at the Armory because he had nowhere else to go. Kris had been at the shelter for three months when Scott arrived. Scott was the typical new guy with the combed hair, flared pants, and tie. He was raw meat in the hands of Kris and his crew. As Kris recalls: "The first thing I thought to myself when I saw him was, 'This guy is soft. We're going to have fun with him.'"

After an initial counseling appointment with Kris, Scott soon found that Kris was too young to stay at the Armory. In defending himself from exile, Kris found that he and Scott had more in common than just a conflict over rules and regulations. They found they had common ground on the subject of music. Kris told him a rhyme and Scott could almost hear the well of verbal talent waiting to be tapped.

As Scott and Kris continued to talk, Kris realized that this man was THE Scott LaRock, his idol and DJ at Broadway International in Harlem. They became the yin and yang of rap. Kris taught Scott about hip-hop from a rapper's view and Scott showed Kris the business side. They formed Boogie Down Productions, named in honor of the borough that had produced them—the Boogie Down Bronx.

BDP distinguished themselves quickly as serious rappers. They didn't succumb to the stereotypical gold-chain-and-Addidas-clad rapper of the hip-hop scene. Their songs centered around the realities of life, which confronted them daily. An unreleased track called "Advance" addressed the nuclear Sword of Damocles over our heads; "Listen to Our Minds" asked us to look beyond skin color and social status; their finest collaboration, "Stop the Violence," was written after Scott and Kris left an ugly scene at a club. Their first album, *Criminal Minded*, did well despite the fact they didn't have a label. Scott didn't care. He was finally doing what he wanted to do; he'd even quit his $23,000-a-year job at the shelter because he believed in BDP.

The record attracted a devoted audience and BDP was going to the top. Tragically, it would be without it's DJ. On a hot August 26, 1987, Scott and four friends drove to the Highbridge Garden Homes in the South Bronx where D-Nice was being harrassed by his girlfriend's jealous ex-boyfriend. When Scott arrived, the boyfriend and his posse were gone, but Scott stayed to talk with some of their friends. As Scott and his friends sat in their jeep, the explosive sound of bullets rang out from across the street. A day later, the man who had stood at his friend's side was no more, his life snuffed out by the work of a "brother."

Who would've thought that despite his talent, Scott would achieve his greatest fame in death.

Maybe in some way, Scott still continues to make music. As long as BDP lives, so does he.

Tracey Lewis,
Spelman College

Students from Washington, D.C., listen to the rappers at the Urban League conference.

THE NATIONAL URBAN LEAGUE EDUCATION INITIATIVE

◆◆◆

The grounds of world leadership and competition are shifting. Tomorrow's world leader won't be the country with the most bombs but the country with the most advanced workers and the most stable social system.

If Congress and the Administration use our strengths and resources wisely, that world leader will be America. The National Urban League is working to help make that happen. We are working to expand opportunities for minorities and to develop America's untapped human resources.

We were the first national organization to focus on the needs of minority children. We were the ones who said that the school reform movement wasn't even talking about the forgotten children of the poor, wasn't even concerned with the aspirations of African-American families.

It was the National Urban League that helped focus the spotlight on the schools our kids go to. And it was the National Urban League—with few resources and an overburdened staff, but with a willing army of volunteers—that launched an Education Initiative to help prepare our children to succeed in this changing world.

Students listening to Stop the Violence members at the conference.

Over 100,000 children and their parents have taken part in some 300 Education Initiative programs conducted in our local Urban Leagues. They're being tutored in science and math, counseled on college admissions, given the support they need to excel in school. One example: in Lansing, Michigan, the black dropout rate is now lower than the white rate, thanks in large part to our efforts.

In some cities, the Urban League was the catalyst for systematic change in the school system. In others, we worked closely with educators to involve parents in their kids' education. In still others, we mobilized coalitions that are making changes in the way the schools serve our children.

The success of the Education Initiative shows what our nationwide network of affiliates and volunteers can do. The Education Initiative is going to have even more impact as we move up the learning curve. We have a panel of distinguished social scientists studying and assessing our efforts. We'll use their study to report to the nation, and then to go forward with programs that reach more of our kids and have even more of an impact on their schools.

Excerpt from an Address by
John E. Jacob, President and Chief
Executive Officer of the National Urban League
August 6, 1989

STATISTICS

Black—and white—poverty increased in the 1980s. Some 8 million more people were poor in 1987 (the last year for which there are definitive figures) than a decade earlier. Two million of the new poor are black. Nearly half of all black children live in poverty. Blacks are three times as likely as whites to be poor.

African-Americans tend to drink more frequently and more heavily during the weekend. Their "heavy drinking" tends to begin in the 20–24 age group and reach a peak in the 35–39 age group. A consequence of this is that African-Americans tend to drink more and for a longer period of time. Subsequently, they are more likely to suffer from the negative consequences of long-term heavy drinking.

The overall effects of alcohol use are catastrophic. Alcoholism is implicated in 70 percent of suicides, 80 percent of homicides, 90 percent of stabbings, and 70 percent of all violent crimes.

♦ A black youth is twice as likely as a white youth to be unemployed. A black college graduate faces about the same odds of unemployment as a white high school graduate who never attended college.

♦ A black male teenager is six times as likely as a white male teenager to be a victim of homicide.

♦ A black child's father is twice as likely as a white child's father to be unemployed. If both parents of a black child work, they can earn 84 percent of what a white family earns.

When compared to youths with above average basic skills, those with the weakest reading and math skills are eight times more likely to have children out of wedlock; nine times more likely to drop out of school before graduation; five times more likely to be out of work and not in school; and four times more likely to be forced to turn to public assistance for basic income support.

My name is Earvin, and my experiences with black-on-black crime have been like a horror story. People kill each other over a word . . .

  If people take the time to stop for a minute and listen to what is happening in the community today, then just maybe people will realize that our brothers and sisters are killing one another. If people would just listen to what these rappers are trying to do, to get people to stop the violence, then we would be better off. It's like a war in our communities today. That's my experience with black-on-black crime and the effects of it.

Earvin M., age 16
Clinton, Michigan

During the sixties in the south, we all stuck together for freedom. We stuck together, using non-violence to get our point across. Dr. Martin Luther King, Jr., one of the great black leaders of the civil rights movement, fought hard for freedom. Malcolm X, the strong Black Muslim leader, gathered many blacks together stressing ''Black Power,'' using force to get their point across . . .

  Today there is a new world with new people. We are fighting, but for no cause. And who are we fighting? Our own people. Why are you killing our own brothers and sisters? If you're not killing our people with guns and other weapons, you're killing them with drugs. Why are you selling drugs to the brother man, to our people? Why are you killing us?

Gary T., age 18
Des Moines, Iowa

ERNIE PANICCIOLI

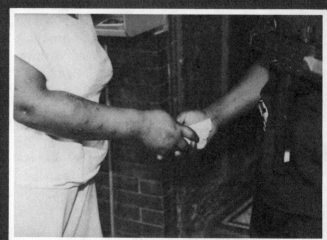
ERNIE PANICCIOLI

There is widespread poverty and unemployment right here in the United States, among blacks and whites. Despite many difficulties and untold disadvantages, our race has come a long way towards self-realization and and fulfillment of individual potentials. We have come far, but we have even farther to go. We must try to build on what has already been achieved so that we can make a better path for future generations to follow.

Black-on-black crime kills everything that dedicated leaders of our race have struggled for and achieved. It creates more obstacles for future generations to overcome, as well as making it extremely difficult for blacks now to improve their lives and their children's chances for a productive and crime-free tomorrow. Almost all of us are eager to work hard for a fuller life and a crime-free tomorrow. There are, unfortunately, some in all races who demand something for nothing and expect everything in life to be handed to them with no effort or sacrifice on their part. Those blacks who want everything without exerting any effort seem to have no conscience, or they pretend to have no conscience and choose to survive by robbery, drug dealing, and other easy-out methods.

Georgette O., age 13
Jacksonville, Florida

The topic of black-on-black crime upsets me to no end. To think that for so many years we were oppressed by the white man and when equality is on the horizon, our own race erupts in total chaos. I was once in a gang, not for the fact that I was tough but because I was young, impressionable, and easily swayed.

Michelle G., age 17
Louisville, Kentucky

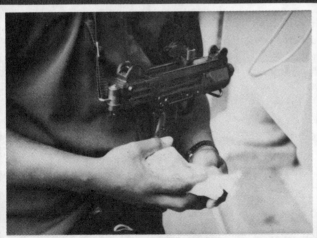

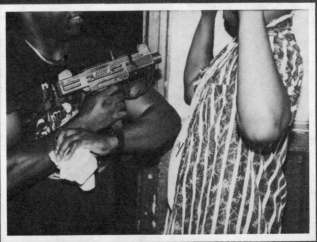

I think that if adults took time to *explain* more to young people, instead of telling them to sit down and shut up, a lot *would* change. Before we learn to deal with racism, we must learn to deal with ourselves . . .

Does rap spark crime? If you don't want to be attacked, then leave your valuables at home. That goes for any public place where there are a lot of people. As for the rappers, not all, but some come on stage like their ready for self-destruction. Most of them have struggled for years to achieve fame, and when they finally get it, they abuse it. To make it even worse, the rappers will even badmouth the audience. The fans have made their fame possible. We got them in the business and we can take them out! Rappers are always boasting about how "bad" they are. That's fine, you're bad. But you don't have to prove it to anyone but yourself! Don't get me wrong, I love rap, but if rappers would stop talking about how bad they are and stop trying to "dis" fellow rappers then maybe rap's image will change.

Latoya S., age 15
East Chicago, Indiana

I am proud of where I come from. But I'm not proud of the black people who give other black people a bad name when they mug, rape, steal, and murder each other. That's not what Dr. Martin Luther King marched and protested for. If he were here today, he'd be appalled at the condition of our world. The evil in some people's hearts is so strong, I wonder if our great leaders died for nothing.

Iyavta M., age 12½
Bronx, New York

Bass to face the fuss that we trust
All of our brothers that can't get enough
Of the violence, supreme idiocy
People on crack, huh, that's wack.
I want to stop the violence
So you won't self-destruct your mind
Thoughts and lots of memories
Held upon me, we have feelings
Of gunmen, drugmen, and policemen.

Anthony M., age 14
Anchorage, Alaska

I recently attended a rap concert with a friend who was into the rap style. Before we left for the show, our friends made sure that we didn't wear any jewelry because theft at concerts was so great. We removed our jewelry before we left. Unfortunately, many concertgoers not privy to this information wore their chains, and many ended up without them. In fact, halfway through the show, a man behind me began to yell, ''My chain's gone! My gold chain!'' He turned around to the man behind him and saw he was wearing a similar chain, so he punched him.

Melissa W., age 17
Louisville, Kentucky

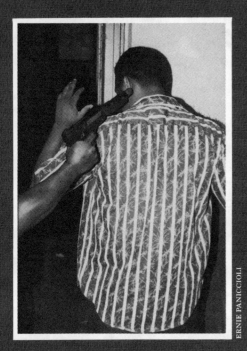

ERNIE PANICCIOLI

Another terrible experience with black-on-black crime that seems to reinforce this sad conclusion was the time outside a rap contest/dance where I was jumped and badly beaten by seven or eight guys for no apparent reason. I know there are those who would contend that I was victimized by my participation in a violent rap music culture. I don't blame rap music for the lack of regard we seem to have for one another. The cause of black-on-black crime like I experienced is much bigger than rap music.

Charles O., age 17
Detroit, Michigan

I think that there are five main causes of black-on-black crime: racism, unemployment, drugs, prisons, and the media. Racism is the bottom line of violence. The majority of offenders are unemployed. Drug addicts and dealers are responsible for much of black-on-black crime. Prisons school inmates in criminal activities and graduate them to greater criminal acts . . .

If offenders thought about the consequences of their crimes, they would stop. The major consequences are: a divided community, disinvestment, and loss of talents. Crime brings mistrust, it drives businesses away, and it is destroying an entire generation of blacks.

Tiesha H., age 15
Deer Park, New York

ERNIE PANICCIOLI

ERNIE PANICCIOLI

▲ *Doug E. Fresh.*
◄ *Al B. Sure!*
▼ *L.L. Kool J and Just-Ice at the STV party.*

ERNIE PANICCIOLI

URBAN LEAGUE CRIME PREVENTION ESSAY CONTEST

PINELLAS COUNTY, FLORIDA

There's a monster on the streets of our community that affects our lives every day. This monster causes hardship, depression, loneliness, and sometimes death. This monster is crime. Our newspapers are polluted with stories about crime. Every night innocent people have to go to sleep worrying about someone coming into their house and hurting them or their family. Today most people accept crime as a part of everyday life. "There's nothing we can do," people say. "It's a hopeless cause."

Actually, there is something we, today's younger generation, can do. As a young citizen, these are things you can do to help prevent crime:

1. Notify the police whenever you see something suspicious. Tell your parents what you saw. Even if they disagree, take charge and call the police; you might prevent a crime.

2. If you have to walk at night, try to go out in groups. Walk in well-lighted areas and carry something to defend yourself (a whistle or a can of mace), just in case.

3. Make other kids aware of the consequences of crime (jail, fines, injury). Help them to understand that crime is like a serious disease that will continue to spread unless we come up with a cure.

4. Help your parents pick out some type of security system. Go with them to the stores. Call other neighbors and ask them what kind of protection they have for their home. Investigate and determine whether or not a guard dog might help.

5. Because we teenagers talk with our friends, we hear certain "happening events," whether it be who said what, or about a robbery or burglary. Although it's not extremely popular, the best thing to do is tell a teacher, parent, or the police.

6. Avoid association with criminals. If enough people follow this advice, crime might disappear.

7. Don't tempt crime to happen. Lock up bikes and don't leave them in the yard without protection. Lock all doors. Don't brag or flash jewelry and money about.

Although these ideas may seem like small details, they can make a significant difference in our neighborhood and our lives. Even if you have never been affected by crime, make it your problem and take on the responsibility to do something about it.

David Valdez, 1st place
(8th grade, Bay Point Middle School)

URBAN LEAGUE CRIME PREVENTION ESSAY CONTEST

PINELLAS COUNTY, FLORIDA

Around the streets of town, in St. Petersburg,
There is crime surrounding us, or haven't you heard?
In the dark alleyways, crimes are being committed,
Misdemeanors or felonies, they must not be permitted!
But these aren't happening just in alleys alone,
In fact, crimes are happening right outside your home.
Don't you go thinkin' these crimes will just dissolve,
If you want to help out, simply don't get involved!
Don't get involved in crime,
It does you no good.
Warn all the people
In your neighborhood.
Lock your garage,
Doors and windows, too.
The next time a crime happens,
It could be aimed at you!
Prowlers everywhere are lookin' all around,
To find a good home to break in and tackle down.
So if you don't want to be a victim of crime,
Lock your house and doors up—listen to this rhyme.
Avoid all hints to others, that you are not home;
If you don't, in your house they will roam.

Even your car is a possible one,
To be vandalized by kids havin' "fun."
So be real careful wherever you park,
Park your car in the sunlight, *not* in the dark!
Lock up the doors and bring in the keys,
By taking these precautions, you will be pleased.
Don't you go thinkin' these crimes will just dissolve,
If you want to help out, simply don't get involved!
Don't get involved in crime,
It does you no good.
Warn all the people
In your neighborhood.
Lock your garage,
Doors and windows too.
The next time a crime happens,
It could be aimed at you!
If you happen to see a crime
Being committed—listen to this rhyme.
Go tell a policeman or dial 911,
This will help stop criminals from havin' "fun"!
Around the streets of town, in St. Petersburg,
There is crime surrounding us, or haven't you heard?
In the dark alleyways crimes are being committed,
Misdemeanors or felonies, they must not be permitted!
Don't you go thinkin' these crimes will just dissolve,
If you want to help out, simply don't get involved!
Don't get involved in crime,
It does you no good.
Tell all the people
In your neighborhood.
Lock your garage,
Doors and windows, too.
The next time a crime happens,
It could be aimed at you!
Word!

Misty Woroner, 3rd place
(8th grade, Southside
Fundamental Middle School)

Kid 'n' Play and Malcolm Warner at the STV party. ▲

Slick Rick and Kool Moe Dee take a break during the shooting of the "Self-Destruction" video. ▶

Malcolm Warner, Kid, Spike Lee, Play, and a friend at a Stop the Violence party. ▼

"**S**elf-destruction" is truly the way to describe America's black society today. We—speaking of this generation—are tomorrow's doctors, lawyers, teachers, and even presidents. Just look at what's happening. I hear people laughing about the future, but it's not laughable. They say they don't want these "crackheads" running America. Well, I say, then why don't you do something about it!

Nakia B., age 14
Jamaica, New York

If these crimes continue, rap artists will not be able to perform. That's not fair to them. Fans like me aren't able to see their favorite stars perform. It just isn't fair . . .

I've only had one experience with black-on-black crime. I saw someone get hurt over gold. Two black men were fighting over a gold chain, which both of them saw at the same time. They had no weapons, luckily. One punched the other until a policeman broke it up. Can you imagine what would have happened if they had weapons?! And all of this for a gold chain. Can you believe it? I think we should all wake up and smell the coffee, because some of us are still sleeping.

Peta-Gaye W., age 12
Bronx, New York

JAMES H. KARALES/MAGNUM PHOTOS

This so-called "rap violence"—you might say it's unconstitutional. You ask why? Because it deprives me and others of our freedom of speech. Just let my father hear me recite a rap from KRS-One or Chuck D, he'll only tell me to shut up . . .

You assume that when you are at a concert with your friends, you have to prove a few things to them. Well, that's what society has put in your small minds. This is what life in urban areas does to us. Corruption is the main thing, and to ruin someone's night would be the perfect event. And who would take the blame? Oh, not you, my friend Violence, but rap music and the industry as a whole. But once your partners are out of the way, your name's relation to the rap world would be eliminated. And who are these partners, you ask? One is inner-city gang members, who not only listen to the music, but also create the violence at concerts. The second is the broadcast and print media who only build your name up and make it more than it really is.

Dewan M., age 17
Lynwood, California

I don't think the tough rap image is the cause of violence. It's just plain violence. Ice-T looks like a pimp on his album cover, but when you listen to what he is saying, like on "Colors," he's saying something positive. He's not like Schooly-D, whose album cover shows him with gold chains and grabbing himself, and the name of his album is *Smoke Some Kill.*

Thomas S., age 16
Suffolk, Virginia

My first experience with black-on-black crime occurred one day when I was hanging out with a group of boys downtown. We were bugging out mildly when we saw a kid come out of a store. One of the boys I was with grabbed the kid and punched him. After that the whole posse rushed him. I admit I hit the boy once before I stopped and turned away. They took the kid's money and ran off. After that incident I decided to try and keep above such things. Now, on reflection, I see that this sort of thing hurts the black community and its reputation. This is a problem which is as bad as drug trafficking. The most I can say is that brothers should put their energy into their schoolwork rather than crime.

Jaja B., age 12
New York, New York

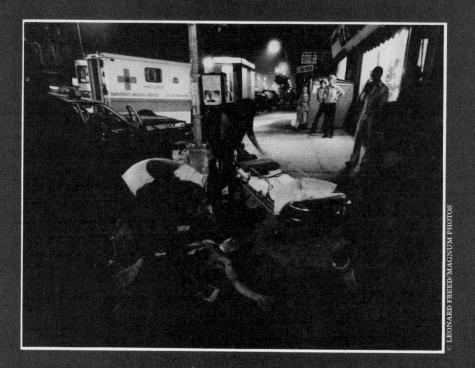

I hate the idea of people being involved in gang activities—like when you fight one person, you fight them all! I just wish it would stop. I mean, it's just useless, it doesn't get people anywhere . . .

I just hope that soon there will be peace among brothers and sisters. But I've realized that it's their lives they're throwing away. If they don't want to stop, then so be it. The only way is to say *no* to violence. WORD!

Saundra P., age 13
Phoenix, Arizona

My experiences with black-on-black crime have been very tragic. Although I have never been directly involved, I've had to watch as well as experience them. The closest and most painful ordeal occurred when my uncle was brutally murdered at the young age of 21, in the hallway of his own home, for reasons I'll probably never know . . .

Black-on-black crime touches my community on a daily basis. On Fridays, when my father leaves for work, we pray that he makes it home safely, considering he's been robbed on a number of occasions. In my neighborhood, on almost every corner, you can find our beautiful black brothers and sisters risking their lives and the lives of others by selling drugs to make a quick buck.

Makeisha W., age 14
Newark, New Jersey

Marley Marl, Big Daddy Kane, and Misha, a hip-hop dancer, talk on the set of "Self-Destruction." ▲

Just-Ice at the video shoot. ▶

M.C. Lyte raps in front of what used to be the famous hip-hop spot the Latin Quarter. ▼

Just before the filming of his performance, Doug E. Fresh stands surrounded by New York's top rap radio personalities. From left to right are Teddy Ted, of the Awesome Two, producer-mixer Marley Marl, Doug E. Fresh, producer-mixer Red Alert, and Special K, of the Awesome Two. ▲

Daddy-O, Chuck D, Nelson George, and KRS-One at the Stop the Violence press conference. ▼

▲ *Chuck D, Fab Five Freddie, and Nelson George carry a coffin, a symbol of the impact of black-on-black crime, across 125th Street.*

▼ *Chuck D, KRS-One, Manhattan State Senator David Paterson, and Doug E. Fresh announce a Rap Against Racism concert to the press. The concert was held in mid-September 1989 in front of the Adam Clayton Powell State Office Building in Harlem.*

KRS-One performs at the ▲
antiracism concert in Harlem.

Kool Moe Dee and Chuck D
perform "Self-Destruction" ▶
together during a concert tour.

My experience with violence occurred when I was over at a friend's house and we were sitting on the porch. As two white men were walking down the street, two black men started after them and decided to have a little fun. They walked up to them and started to beat them up. The black guys walked away laughing and slapping hands. Just seeing that made me want to cry.

La Kieshia T., age 14
Youngstown,Ohio

Since the punishment for black-on-black crime is less than punishment for black-on-white or white-on-white, the "system" makes black-on-black crime more attractive—almost invitational.

Sarina W., age 12
Columbus, Ohio

There were two guys who had an earlier confrontation and decided to end it once and for all. They fought until one guy pulled out a knife and killed the other—my friend Corey. I hope I never have to witness such a brutal incident like that ever again.

Omar R., age 15
New York, New York

I have had a lot of experience with black-on-black crime. I live in Detroit, and there are drugs and crime everywhere here. My boyfriend and I were driving down the street as two guys in a car pulled up beside us. One of them started to talk to me. I ignored him until we came to a red light. I looked back and saw they had pulled out guns and pointed them at us. My boyfriend managed to dodge them before they could shoot. Now whenever anyone pulls up beside me, I am frightened . . .

My cousin was killed on October 25, 1988, by gunfire. He was shot in the head. His girlfriend was with him and they shot her in the mouth. Thank God she did not die. The guys that did it are in jail; one of them got twenty to forty years . . .

My best friend's boyfriend is in jail for selling drugs. He hasn't been sentenced yet. In 1987, my boyfriend was shot by two females on his way to the prom. So, as you can see, I've had enough experience with black-on-black crime, and I am sick to death of it.

Tracy R., age 18
Detroit, Michigan

STATISTICS

Among younger black men (the under-30 group starting families) real income is half what it was in the early 1970s. A prime cause is the extraordinarily high black unemployment rate—about two and a half times that of whites, and increasing.

Clearly, illegal drug use is either directly or indirectly related to much of the crime that plagues the black community. According to a 1986 National Institute on Drug Abuse study of drug-related deaths in 27 metropolitan areas across the country, blacks accounted for 25 percent of the victims.

♦ While whites are more vulnerable than blacks to personal theft, blacks are more vulnerable than whites to violent crimes.

♦ Blacks have the highest victimization rates for rape, robbery, and assault.

♦ The average American has a 1-in-133 chance of being murdered. However, for black males in America, the chances are 1-in-21.

♦ Most violent crimes against blacks are committed by black offenders (84 percent).

♦ Blacks are more likely to be victims of violent crime than whites or members of other racial groups.

According to a Census Bureau Report on Family Income, the poverty rate for whites decreased between 1986 and 1987 while for blacks it increased and the rate for persons of other races and Hispanics did not change significantly. In 1987, 10.5 percent of whites were below the poverty level, down from 11 percent in 1986. For blacks, the poverty rate was 33.1 percent in 1987, up 2 percent from 1986. In 1987, the poverty rate for Hispanics was 28.2 percent and for persons of other races 18.3 percent.

A SURVIVAL CURRICULUM FOR INNER-CITY KIDS

by KRS-ONE

Young black New Yorkers are raised in a racially polarized society. The murder in Bensonhurst of Yusuf Hawkins is not an isolated incident. The number of racially motivated crimes has escalated since Howard Beach, as the city's mayoral candidates ought to know. And these crimes are only the most obvious form of racism.

Young black kids experience a more subtle form of racism when their heritage and culture are stripped from them early on in their schooling. While no single cause accounts for the problems of inner-city kids, much of what black youth is missing—self-esteem, creative opportunity, outlook, goals—can be traced to what we're not learning in schools.

If more creative effort and dedication is not put toward educating the large, vital, and energetic populace that is this city's black youth, the city may soon be consumed by the symptoms of racism, and an already polarized New York may tear itself apart.

In the city's schools, Afro-American kids are taught white American history, while our own heritage is blatantly ignored. Everyone is supposed to learn about being (white) Americans. As I say in my song "Why is that?" It's like trying to teach a dog to be a cat.

I was homeless for seven years. My mother, a single parent, was overwhelmed with responsibility. Her uncertainty about the future created unbearable pressure at home. I ran away at the age of 13 to live an even more uncertain life, bouncing from park to subway to shelter. But at least I was in control.

The lessons they were teaching in school—Thomas Jefferson, the Civil War, etc.—left me empty. Aggravated at what I was expected to learn, I was even more aggravated that I wasn't even being taught what I desperately wanted to know.

Most of what I know of myself and my culture, the things I try to bring across in my songs, I picked up either in conversation with enlightened adults or through my own study. I took to the public libraries for shelter, but I came out with much more.

Daddy-O, Chuck D. KRS-One, and Just-Ice at the STV press conference.

If my story has a happy ending, it is the exception. Most people refuse to understand that black inner-city youth, alienated by their schooling, are left with nothing else to grab onto. Outside of the classroom, they are at the mercy of government cutbacks of much needed youth programs. The R.I.F. (Reading Is Fundamental) truck doesn't come around to poor areas anymore; it has been replaced by the ice cream truck, followed closely by the paddy wagon.

Ineffectively schooled, with no positive role models, just wanting money like fantasy people on TV, poor youth have nothing constructive to do. When Nancy Reagan told everyone to "just say no" to drugs, she didn't indicate what to say "yes" to. We are adrift in this country, exiles from a system that wants nothing to do with us. Many of us will continue to end up on drugs, in jail, or dead.

I have little faith in political solutions. I'm not alone. How can politicians from privileged backgrounds ever understand life in the ghetto? It's easy for them to cut social programs without a second thought. Those politicians—especially minorities—who come out of poor backgrounds have to compromise themselves so much to get elected that they forget where they've come from.

Can things change? Revamping the school system to educate all students would be the first step. But it must happen on several levels.

In addition to providing Afro-American history classes for all students, schools also have to teach the ABCs of how to survive in the system. Why is the flashy drug dealer the neighborhood role model? Kids should be taught how some South American farmers are dying on their plantations because they don't want to give up their coca leaf cash crops. Maybe they'll think twice about how Johnny on the corner gets his money. Maybe they'll make other choices.

The spark to learn of oneself must originate somewhere. The schools have been ineffectual, but the outlook is not entirely bleak.

Rap music, stigmatized by many as mindless music having no artistic or socially redeeming value, can be a means to change. Last fall, I helped create the Stop the Violence Movement, a collective of rap artists and music industry figures who are speaking out against the evils of black-on-black crime. We donated about $150,000—the proceeds from an all-star rap single entitled ''Self-Destruction''—to the National Urban League to fund Stop the Violence programs to combat illiteracy and crime in the inner city.

This could be part of a larger trend. I teach a new fad in my songs: intelligence. It's no longer acceptable to strut around with big gold chains, boasting. That stereotype, that lifestyle, must be crushed.

Maybe the message is getting through—black kids in the streets are starting to wear African medallions in place of the chains. It's just a small gesture, but it indicates that awareness and pride in our heritage is starting to take hold.

Politicians, school board officials: Take a good long look at what's being taught in schools. Does it really make sense? Does it help promote co-existence? Know this: If you strip away the identity of a child, he is left with nothing. That vacuum is filled by the surrounding environment. If his environment is cold-blooded, negative, and violent, he becomes cold-blooded, negative, and violent.

From the New York Times, *September 9, 1989.*

Hanging out at the Urban League conference are Jazzy Jordan, Ann Carli, Nelson George, Chuck D, ▶ *D-Nice, Daddy-O, Darryl Clark, M.C. Lyte, and Delite.*

This check for $180,000 represents the Stop the Violence Movement's first contribution to the National Urban League. Left to right are Kevin Gibbs ▼ *of the Urban League, Nelson George, Frank Lomax III, also of the Urban League, and RCA's Jazzy Jordan and Darryl Clark*

TAMARA

M.C. Lyte raps at the National Urban League conference in Washington, D.C.

My name is Tamara, but some call me Tammy
I pop some PCP to keep from getting clammy
I close the door because I know I'm gonna
Smoke some ganja, weed, a marijuana
Of course I'm fly, because I get high
My eyes get red, dizzy is my head
And when people are talking I don't know what's said
Of course it's dangerous, it couldn't be right
But I'll meet right here same time tomorrow night
And just to show I'm tough, I'll do the white stuff
My nose will get numb, Hey you want some
You take a little hit, and you'll be just as dumb
Cause when I was younger I used to pop my veins
Any type of drug to take away the pain
Inflicted on me when I was beaten as a child
Believe me when I tell you my household was wild
Sexually molested by an overworked father
I said I'd tell mom, he said don't bother
She won't listen, he was telling the truth
So I'd sometimes cry with the pigeons on the roof
And every marking period I'd fail my class
And every marking period my parents kicked my ass
I used to hang out in the buildings that were abandoned
My soul was lost, my spirit was stranded
I guess I would have prayed but I didn't know how

I always wondered how people got the holy ghost and went to church
But I was so drugged up I couldn't even search for the answer
But every now and then I'd take some Mescaline
And in between that time I'd take a little heroin
It was a cool hangout kick, till I got hooked just like a crook
Just say drugs and I click and shake
Like an earthquake is just about to happen
You say needle and I'm slappin' my arm
Cause I'm an addict, a fiend, a fanatic
Unclean drugs are my theme—It's like a capital—
Drugs—I often wonder how I got in this mess
But it's evident I use drugs to escape
The brutality, also the rape
I tried more than once to commit suicide
I closed my eyes, balled my hand into a fist
Took a razor and I slit my wrist
The ambulance came right away
I stayed in the asylum day after day
The garbage they gave us, not a word was said
See, cause if you talked you wouldn't get fed
Attempted suicide was why I was there
One girl strangled her mom and set fire to her hair
My parents came and got me, I don't know why
Three days went by and I was just as high
Once again I did something dumb
I got involved in prostitution because drugs I needed some
Don't know the father but gave birth to a son
The doctor said there'd be no more, so he's the only one
Fifteen years later my son's a hooligan
It's a pity to say, but it's a hereditary sin
It came to the point he got arrested about two times a week
Sticking up his victims on poorly lit streets
What made me mad, what was so damn sad
He used drugs like it was a fad
He walked around with a temper like a time bomb
I said why son why
He said I learned it from you, mom . . .

M.C. Lyte

A slew of rappers together on the morning of the video shoot.

YOU MUST LEARN

If you are a young African-American, nothing in this book has surprised you. You already know that rap music is a powerful expression of your culture, of the world that surrounds you—and sometimes traps you. And you already know about the drug-culture violence and the racism that are so often roadblocks to your future.

So for you, this book is a document of a place in time. Years from now when people hear the record "Self-Destruction" and read the words of pain and pride related here by your peers, they'll say, "That's what it was like in the 1980s."

The question you should ask now is not "What happens next?" but "How can I shape the future—*my* future?" Because the Stop the Violence Movement is about participating, being an active force in your own life.

Number one is, you must arm yourself—not with a knife or a gun, but with the arsenal of your mind. Intelligence is not a new fad, it's your future. If school is "boring" or your teacher is "weak," then load up outside the classroom. The Stop the Violence reading lists provided by Chuck D, KRS-One, and myself are purposefully "Afrocentric," which means they reflect a black view of the world, as written by African-American writers.

Hey, I'm not advocating that you dismiss your school or your teacher. No way. What I'm saying is, that in the classroom or in your room, you have to seek out information aggressively. If you're slow you'll blow. If you wait you'll be more than late. You'll be ignorant, an economic liability, both to yourself and your community. If for some reason you don't want to read, there are tapes, records, radio shows, and other materials out there about the African experience in Africa and America.

Complaining about racism is fine. As Chuck D said, "You gotta fight the powers that be." There will be times in your life—hopefully not many—when you'll have to be as bold as the Freedom Riders, who risked death so that *all* people could eat, sleep, and vote wherever they wished in America. But intelligence, a by-product of information, is how you'll earn a living in the '90s and beyond. Listen. There are no old crack-dealers and no old crack-heads. Believe it. So if you're contemplating that as a career option, so long.

Only through "the word" will enlightenment come. Be it the Bible, the Koran, the *Wall Street Journal*, *Spiderman*, or *Essence*, you must read. By the time you enter your senior year of high school, if you don't understand why Booker T. Washington, W.E.B. DuBois, Malcolm X, Marcus Garvey, A. Philip Randolph, Whitney Young, Huey Newton, or Duke Ellington are important—then *you must learn*.

What does this have to do with stopping self-destruction? As a young person you can't control the flow of drugs, the prevalence of guns, racism, or poverty in America. Adults have to take full responsibility for those evils. But if you want to prepare yourself to stop the violence, you must learn. If you want to change things, you must learn. Don't be seduced by quick, deadly money. It's real simple: You must learn.

Nelson George

NELSON GEORGE'S READING LIST

Hard Road to Glory by Arthur Ashe
  A three-volume history of black athletes in America

Eyes on the Prize by Juan Williams
  An illustrated history of the civil rights movement

Mama by Terry McMillan
  A novel about a mother's relationship with her children

Blues People by Leroi Jones
  A provocative view of jazz and blues, from slavery until the 1960s

Spike Lee's Gotta Have It by Spike Lee
  The story behind the young filmmaker's breakthrough film
  She's Gotta Have It

Ma Rainey's Black Bottom; Fences; Joe Turner's Come and Gone
  by August Wilson. Three award-winning plays by America's
  premiere African-American playwright

Black Boy by Richard Wright
  An autobiography of the writer's youth

The Langston Hughes Reader by Langston Hughes
  A collection of essays, fiction, and poetry by the distinguished
  writer

The Color Purple by Alice Walker
  The controversial and poetic novel

Bloods by Wallace Terry
   An oral history of the Vietnam War by black veterans
When and Where I Enter by Paula Giddings
   A history of African-American women's many roles
   in American life
The Autobiography of Malcolm X
   The story of the slain leader, co-written by Alex Haley

PUBLIC ENEMY'S READING LIST

From Slavery to Freedom by John Hope Franklin

Message to the Black Man by Elijah Muhammad

The Destruction of Black Civilization by Chancellor Williams

Part of My Soul Went with Him by Winnie Mandela

Women in Islam by Tynetta Muhammed

How Europe Underdeveloped Africa by Walter Rodney

The Iceman Inheritance by Michael Bradley

How to Eat to Live by Elijah Muhammad

What They Never Taught You in History Class by J. A. Rogers

Tougher Than Leather: The Authorized Biography of RUN-DMC
   by B. Adler

BOOGIE DOWN PRODUCTIONS' READING LIST

Blacks in Science by Ivan Von Sertima

Hills of Africa by Kwame Nkrumah

How Europe Underdeveloped Africa by Walter Rodney

The West and the Rest of Us by Chinweizu

The African Origin of Civilization: Myth or Reality
   by Cheikh Anta Diop

The Destruction of Black Civilization by Chancellor Williams

The Pleasures of Philosophy by Will Durant

Chakras and Esoteric Healing by Zachary F. Lansdowne

From Babylon to Timbuktu by Rudolf R. Windsor

Metaphysics, the Science of Life by Anthony J. Fisichella

If you want to find out more about what you can do to help stop the violence, you can call the Urban League affiliate nearest you.

NATIONAL URBAN LEAGUE

500 East 62nd Street
New York, NY 10021

Local Affiliates

ALABAMA

    Birmingham (205) 326-0162

ARIZONA

    Phoenix (602) 254-5611

    Tucson (602) 791-9522

ARKANSAS

    Little Rock (501) 372-3037

CALIFORNIA

    Los Angeles (213) 299-9660

    Oakland (415) 839-8011

    Sacramento (916) 739-0627

    San Diego (619) 263-3115

    San Jose (408) 286-8665

    Santa Ana (714) 558-7996

COLORADO

    Colorado Springs (303) 634-1525

    Denver (303) 388-5861

CONNECTICUT

    Hartford (203) 527-0147

    New Haven (203) 624-4168

    Stamford (203) 327-5810

DISTRICT OF COLUMBIA

    Washington (202) 265-8200

FLORIDA

    Fort Lauderdale (305) 584-0777

    Jacksonville (904) 356-8336

    Miami (305) 696-4450

    Orlando (407) 841-7654

    St. Petersburg (813) 327-2081

    Tallahassee (904) 222-6111

    Tampa (813) 229-8117

    West Palm Beach (305) 833-1461

GEORGIA

    Albany (912) 883-1410

    Atlanta (404) 659-1150

    Columbus (404) 323-3687

ILLINOIS

Alton (618) 463-1906
Aurora (312) 820-8030
Champaign (217) 356-1364
Chicago (312) 285-5800
Peoria (309) 673-7474
Springfield (217) 789-0832
Waukegan (312) 249-3770

INDIANA

Anderson (317) 649-7126
Fort Wayne (219) 424-6326
Gary (219) 887-9621
Indianapolis (317) 639-9404
Marion (317) 664-3933
South Bend (219) 287-7261

KANSAS

Wichita (316) 262-2463

KENTUCKY

Lexington (606) 233-1561
Louisville (502) 776-4622

LOUISIANA

New Orleans (504) 524-4667

MARYLAND

Baltimore (301) 523-8150

MASSACHUSETTS

Boston (617) 266-3550
Springfield (413) 739-7211

MICHIGAN

Battle Creek (616) 962-5553
Detroit (313) 832-4600
Flint (313) 239-5111

Grand Rapids (616) 245-2207
Lansing (517) 487-3608
Muskegon (616) 722-3736
Pontiac (313) 335-8730

MINNESOTA

Minneapolis (612) 521-1099
St. Paul (612) 224-5771

MISSISSIPPI

Jackson (601) 362-6536

MISSOURI

Kansas City (816) 471-0550
St. Louis (314) 371-0040

NEBRASKA

Omaha (402) 453-9730

NEW JERSEY

Elizabeth (201) 351-7200
Englewood (201) 568-4988
Jersey City (201) 451-8888
Morristown (201) 539-2121
Newark (201) 624-6660
Trenton (609) 393-1512

NEW YORK

Albany (518) 463-3121
Binghamton (607) 723-7303
Buffalo (716) 854-7625
Melville (516) 691-7230
New York (212) 730-5200
Rochester (716) 325-6530
Syracuse (315) 472-6955
White Plains (914) 428-6300

NORTH CAROLINA

Charlotte (704) 376-9834

Winston-Salem (919) 725-5614

OHIO

Akron (216) 434-3101

Canton (216) 456-3479

Cincinnati (513) 721-2237

Cleveland (216) 421-0999

Columbus (614) 221-0544

Dayton (513) 220-6650

Elyria (216) 323-3364

Massillon (216) 833-2804

Springfield (513) 323-4603

Warren (216) 394-4316

Youngstown (216) 788-6533

OKLAHOMA

Oklahoma City (405) 424-5243

Tulsa (918) 584-0001

OREGON

Portland (503) 280-2600

PENNSYLVANIA

Harrisburg (717) 234-5925

Lancaster (717) 394-1966

Philadelphia (215) 476-4040

Pittsburgh (412) 261-1130

Sharon (412) 981-5310

RHODE ISLAND

Providence (401) 351-5000

SOUTH CAROLINA

Columbia (803) 799-8150

Greenville (803) 242-1640

TENNESSEE

Chattanooga (615) 756-1762

Knoxville (615) 524-5511

Memphis (901) 327-3591

Nashville (615) 329-2575

TEXAS

Austin (512) 478-7176

Dallas (214) 421-5361

Houston (713) 526-5127

VIRGINIA

Norfolk (804) 627-0864

Richmond (804) 649-8407

WASHINGTON

Seattle (206) 461-3792

Tacoma (206) 383-2006

WISCONSIN

Madison (608) 251-8550

Milwaukee (414) 374-5850

Racine (414) 637-8532